# TRY BEING IN OUR SHOES

## CHRISTINE REDA

Copyright @2021 by Christine Reda

All rights reserved. No part of this book may be reproduced in any form or by any electronic or mechanical means, including information storage and retrieval systems, without permission in writing from the publisher, except by reviewers, who may quote brief passages in a review.

This publication contains the opinions and ideas of its author. It is intended to provide helpful and informative material on the subjects addressed in the publication. The author and publisher specifically disclaim all responsibility for any liability, loss or risk, personal or otherwise, which is incurred as a consequence, directly or indirectly, of the use and application of any of the contents of this book.

WORKBOOK PRESS LLC
187 E Warm Springs Rd,
Suite B285, Las Vegas, NV 89119, USA

| | |
|---|---|
| Website: | https://workbookpress.com/ |
| Hotline: | 1-888-818-4856 |
| Email: | admin@workbookpress.com |

Ordering Information:
Quantity sales. Special discounts are available on quantity purchases by corporations, associations, and others. For details, contact the publisher at the address above.

| | |
|---|---|
| ISBN-13: | 978-1-954753-50-1 (Paperback Version) |
| | 978-1-954753-51-8 (Digital Version) |

REV. DATE: 18.02.2021

## *Dedicated*

To my three sons, Alex, Philip, and Anthony.

Mom would like to say, if you put your mind to something, you can reach your dream, no matter how big or small it might seem. Follow through, and the result will be your success. I have learned that later on in life and though I never in a million years thought I would have a book published because, growing up I was not interested in reading or writing. The years passed on, and I became more confident, positive, and so adventurous and decided to write an inspiring book. Hope you enjoy the book as much as I did writing it.

Love always,
Mom

## Dear Readers,

After republishing my book "Try being in Our shoes" an unexpected loss happened in my life. My eldest son Alex has passed away. He left behind a wife and two children. I was in total shock for a very long time. Trying to be strong for his wife, my two grandkids, and the whole family. The struggles go on every day. I do get up every morning, I do the best that I can. Their children are 17 and 14 now and reminds me of when my father passed away. I was my granddaughters age.

There are other family mentioned in this book that have passed away. My mom which every day I try calling her and it saddens me especially around the holidays, when I'm trying to cook and want to ask her for advice because she was the best cook! My mother in law lived a long life into her 90's sadly left us this year RIP. It's been awhile since my sister Fran left us, but it seems Like yesterday. My son Anthony's dog Ryder, who was a big part of my life, had to be put down. I still feel his loss. I feel their energy to give me the strength to get through each day. I hope when you read this book you will get some things out of this short, easy read book to help you get through your darkest moments. On A positive note my son Philip and his wife Meagan have a son named Zane and they are expecting in January a little girl Alexia Rose Reda, my youngest son Anthony married a beautiful young lady lundyn which they just had an active, smiley baby boy Axyl Walker Reda. I am truly blessed! Remember there will be sunshine with a rainbow so keep the faith and stay positive. Things will get better if you have that mindset. That's how I live every day and I hope you enjoy my book. God bless you all.

## Introduction

This winter has been very challenging due to all the snow, resulting in me being stuck in the house. I decided after reading a few books that I should write a book about myself and my family that would interest others. This book would be good for all ages to read.

*I* was born on October 12, 1958, and I have three older sisters and a younger brother. My grandparents lived in the apartment above us. They watched us a lot because my dad owned a luncheonette with his brother, and mom used to help my dad when his brother was off. We lived in Yonkers, New York, and went to a Catholic elementary school. Since I was the youngest, I always followed my sisters. All three sisters were always there for me. They would help me with homework and studying for tests.

I got hit by a car in the fourth grade and I was in the hospital for a long time. I was bleeding internally, and had other complications. I missed too much school work which, unfortunately led me to retain the grade. When I returned to school the following school year, I was still on the fourth-grade line; all the kids were staring and screaming, "You are on the wrong line!" The teacher came to me and knew right away what was going on. She took me inside so I could get myself together. The days went on it got easier to go to school. Due to the trauma and severity of the car accident, I had a learning disability, which affected my reading, writing, etc. This resulted to low self-esteem. Having a disability was a big disadvantage, so no matter what disadvantages you come across don't give up and let time heal.

When my brother was born, all attention was on him. Sometimes I felt like I was alone, although I had other siblings that were several years older than me. They were fine with having a little brother around. Three years later, after my brother was born my father passed away. This left my mother with five children. I was a rebellious teenager, always acting out from my father's death, and all the attention was on my little brother which now, I understand why. I would run away, hang out with the wrong crowd, not listen to my mom or anyone, for that matter. When you lose someone close to you it is very easy to rebel and not listen. By doing that you are only making it worse on yourself. Looking back I wish I knew that, so doing the right thing and not rebelling helps you get stronger.

After finding myself, which took a few years, I didn't want to go to school anymore, although my family would tell me it's a must to go to school but, I didn't listen. My sister Vicki went to college, and she would take me to class with her so I would learn to like school. She tried very hard to convince me to stay in school. I told her I wasn't going back to school anymore. I would find a job. I liked college better than I liked high school. She replied that I needed to finish high school before starting college. Although I did not finish high school, I soon realized the importance of having a diploma and went back to fill that void.

I was riding on a bus to go to the mall and ran into an old friend. We got to talking, and I told her I need a job. She said that I would have to fill out an application and she would refer me. I filled out the application, and a week later, I got a call to go on an interview. United Parcel was the company where I was hired, and I worked there for a few years.

Then, I met my husband. We went out for several months then broke up. After a year we met again at Lawrence Hospital. He was in the emergency room with his mom, and I was there for my knee. Ever since that day we have been together. I always knew we would meet again.

I was modeling for a few years when I fell in love with Johnny; however modeling didn't sit well with him. We lived with each other at a very young age. We had a broken table to eat on, wobbly chairs, and a mattress to sleep on the floor. The little money we had we bought a living room set. Living with each other was a challenge due to the immaturity of our age. My mom paid for the wedding, and everyone said it was the most elegant wedding that they had been to in years. We both said to each other that if we survived our first year we can get through anything. Next thing we knew we were married. We continued on a rough and rocky road. We were trying to get through all our problems before we had our son Alex. We still had some problems after he was born that needed to be ironed out. Two years later, we had a second son named Philip. I wish I could tell you that we had our shit together but, we weren't even close. Seven years later, we were blinded with another boy named Anthony. I was pregnant with twins at the time, however lost one of the babies in the fourth month. We loved our sons and did everything to make our marriage work. Having my three sons made me realize it didn't matter if our shit was together or not as long as we were together everything was ok.

My son Alex and his wife, Lisa, lived with us they had their first child living under our roof. We were so excited knowing that we were becoming first time grandparents. It was a special time for the family. They had a boy and they named him Alexander. Three years later, they had another child, and it was a beautiful girl named Arielle. This time they had their child under their own roof.

My son Philip got married to his High School sweetheart, Meagan. Now, I am blessed with two daughter–in–laws that are like daughters to me.

My third son Anthony is dating his childhood friend. I am very excited for Anthony is continuing to college and achieve all his endeavors in life.

On January 28, 2008 the day that I lost my house to a horrific fire it seemed like it was the end of the world for me. I could only imagine the sea of flames and all the memories being burnt down in my house. My husband, sons and daughter in law Lisa arrived on the scene experiencing the fire first hand. I was working at a retail store at the time of the fire. How ironic is this, as they were dealing with the fire, I was dealing with a robbery at work. My husband called me with the terrible news but I was unable to leave due to the robbery. I had to go to the police department and give a statement for the police report. The only good thing was the police located the suspect and arrested him. On the ride home from work all I could think about was what is my family going to do. All I could do was cry hysterical and pray that my family and I would have the strength for this long distressing road ahead of us. The fire departments came from all over the different counties to try to save our house. When the fire seemed like it was controlled it would ignite again. It took a while for the fire to be extinguished. The only way we got through this disaster was the fact that no one was hurt or killed. I thank the lord every day for that and take every day as a blessing. It took several years to rebuild and get into our new house. We built on the same property, however in a different spot. Finally this horrific day was coming to an end. We all were clueless on what we were going to do, let alone where we were going to sleep. Thankfully my son Alex and Lisa opened their home for our family to sleep.

The house was overcrowded with my husband and I on one side of the basement and Philip and Anthony at the other. Upstairs was Alex and Lisa along with their two children. The sad emotions over our heads a couple days later our friends and family from all over gave us clothes and money to help us in this time of need. I often found myself reminiscing about positive memories to pass time. For an example my son Philip was living with us before the fire and had a beautiful bedroom upstairs that he had recently fixed up into a living space with its own deck entrance. Now Anthony's room I thought about often because we also recently converted our two bedrooms upstairs in to one large bedroom. I will always have the image of his face when we finished his room. It was completely filled with happiness. These memories did help me because I could not wait to make new memories in our new house. I started to envision my new house being built and started thinking about all the things I could do to make my family feel that special home feeling they once had. As much as I tried to stay positive with all those memories it was very easy to fall off track with the negatives. My husband and I did multiple renovations to the house prior to the fire. I was so devastated simply at the fact that we did so much to our home and it was taken before we even had a chance to enjoy it. As time went on Philip and Anthony were lucky enough to be welcomed in to their significant others homes.

Philip went and stayed with his girlfriend Meagan at her parent's Rob and Judy's house. Rob and Judy really took a great amount of pressure off my husband and I because we were constantly worrying about where Philip was going to stay. I see Rob and Judy as a godsend and not only friends but family. Anthony stayed with his girlfriend at that time and her parents, Theresa and Eddie. I will always be thankful and love them for having him stay with them in a time of need, especially because Anthony was getting ready to go off to college.

Anthony went away to college early for his football camp at Wesley College in Delaware. He came home one weekend and said he wanted a dog. A few months later, he bought a puppy boxer and named him Ryder. Ryder grew up at my son's college house. I heard many stories of Ryder getting into some mischief as they did. Two years later Anthony transferred to Mercy College and received his Bachelor Degree. Anthony went on job interviews that frustrated him. He decided to stay and help his dad grow his moving company with his brothers and make a living. Ryder was a companion for Anthony when he went away to school. College is a big step to take and can be lonely being away from family and friends. Now that I am not working, I am home with him a lot. As a result of being home I am beginning to get that companionship my son shared with him. Ryder looks at me with his large brown eyes and floppy ears when I head to the door. He bolts to the door and knows automatically that I am going to take him for a ride every time I grab my key. He helps my errands go fast and smooth. I enjoy his company and he puts a smile on my face.

We bought an old yacht to live on at the Hudson River in Newburgh, New York. My husband and I would have wound up in an asylum because we were under a lot of stress and pressure from having lost our home. The only good thing was we both had jobs to keep us busy. It was very mentally upsetting and draining, separating from our kids to live elsewhere, even though they were safe and had a roof over their head. The view of the mountains and water was very calming to us; it got us through.

Now we have rebuilt, and living in the new house. The house is much bigger and different from our other one. My husband and I didn't have the money to buy new furniture for the house. My mother gave us the money, and we paid her back a little at a time. My sister Lucille and her husband Will were very generous and gave us a gift to help out with what we needed for the house. One day, I was trying to figure out what we needed for the house. I said "Are you kidding? We need everything." We tried to keep the cost down; it still was a small fortune to furnish the house.

My health was always challenging, with asthma and a paralyzed diaphragm. Most people would take a few days to feel better. It would take me a couple of weeks, or be hospitalized. My condition got worse and the medicine I take has side effects. I have gained weight, feel jumpy at times and moody. I have learned to control my eating. Also eating healthier food and exercising. I am learning to stay calm and deal with things. When you think positive your mind and health will follow.

I worked over twenty-five years. Last year in 2014, I got sick and was hospitalized. I was admitted for seven days having difficult time breathing and other symptoms. Once

I thought I was feeling better, I went back to work and realized I could not do my job anymore. The company I was working for said there were no jobs available in retail to accommodate my disability.

Prior to working retail, I was working with autistic children. It was a great, challenging job with a lot of meaning working with them. I was thankful for every day I was working with those beautiful children and went home to appreciate my own kids.

The winter of 2014-2015 was a record breaker for all the snow we had in twenty–five years. I stayed home and learned how to crochet, made some scarves and hats for my family. Eventually, I got bored with that, so I moved on to taking yoga and painting classes. The yoga class helped me with my breathing and strengthening. I like this class it keeps me calm and grounded. The painting class is very advanced, and there are some fine artists in my class. I learned a lot and I am able to paint by myself.

When my son Alex was born, he was the first grandchild on my husband's side of the family. My in-laws spoiled him in the most compassionate, loving way. They would always love to show him off. They showed so much interest and could not help enough. My son Alex remembers his poppy (grandfather). Alex was in third grade when poppy passed away. I spoke to his teacher and told her what was happening, and she said that explained why Alex forgot his lines in the play. We should have called the teacher, but with all the commotion, I thought it would be better to tell her in person. My son Philip was in the first grade and Anthony was an infant. My in-laws cared for my boys and showed them much love. I cannot understand why people complain about their in-laws because I had the best.

When my sons were in school I was very overprotective and eager for them to receive the best education and keep them in sports. Alex decided he wanted to use his knowledge after finishing school and partnered with his dad in the family business. Philip manages one of the buildings for our family business. He is working diligently and generating more work to help grow the business. Anthony is working efficiently setting up new jobs, coming up with strategies for getting work and staying productive. My husband, John started this business and is a good man, a hard worker, has a big heart. He gave the boys a start in the business, and they are running with it. We are very proud of them.

When my son Philip, and Meagan were planning their wedding, they knew we didn't have that much money. We figured out a plan so that we can help pay for some of the expenses. I did not want them to lose out because of our loss. We did the best, and they were very appreciative. They had a wonderful wedding. My son had both brothers to be his best man. Alex and Anthony both had an outstanding speech for Philip on his special day.

My perception of my childhood now is a child that lost her father at such an early age had problems dealing with the loss. My mom also, was having a difficult time grieving over the loss of her husband. My brother was young in age not to realize we lost our dad but certainly remembers him. However my sisters dealt with their loss differently. It wasn't expressed at the time only their actions showed the love that they had for mom and me by taking care of us and helping us cope.

I did learn that she is a great mom and I didn't see it till later on when I had children of my own and I learned that my mom is a very strong woman for raising five children alone. I am truly my mother's daughter. Mom is eighty- four and looks great besides having problems with her legs and walking.

My mother lives in Florida; I talk to her almost every day and see her two or three times a year.

The birthday of Anthony, is February26, and so is my mom's. I will never forget, when I was in the hospital, mom came running in saying, "My daughter is having a baby on my birthday". Every birthday they share together is very special to me.

I enjoyed writing my first inspirational book. As I wrote this book I was able to reflect on some of my past memories which molded me into the woman I am today. I learned from them and when you read this book, I hope you will be entertained. Although, at times you may think you are the only one experiencing a set back you have to realize that others are experiencing hardships as well. If you open up and talk about what is going on in your life, you will find yourself at ease. You will release your anxiety. Also learn about yourself and how you can control your future. I felt lost, confused and scared, I stepped back to weigh my thoughts and I figured out how smart it was to turn my thoughts around from negative to positive. If you give up on yourself you will never know the outcome of happiness and being in control. My family and I literally went through a lot of high and lows in life. If my family was able to perceive their thoughts and turn hardships into a learning tool then you can take whatever life throws your way and put it in your own book.

Going to my baptism with my mother and sisters Fran, Lucille and Vicki (from left to right).

My grandma and grandpa.

It was always fun being with my dad. We always were doing fun things like swimming and going on vacation.

This is a picture of me vacationing at the beach with my family.

Me at age ten on a family trip.

My wish came true Christmas Day when I got a new bike.

Puerto Rico with my family.

Enjoying the outdoor life in the country.
The land my husband and I bought together.

Enjoying some music.

My in-Laws

My house where my family and I lived for twelve years.
(1996-2008) before fire.

A sideview of our house where my family and I lived for twelve years.
(1996-2008) before fire.

This is the Yacht we bought to live on at the Hudson River in Newburgh, New York, while our house was being built.

Ryder

This is our new home, we waited for it to be built.

Enjoying Easter with our family.

www.ingramcontent.com/pod-product-compliance
Lightning Source LLC
Chambersburg PA
CBHW072040080526
44578CB00007B/541